MW01173179

The Idea Execution Playbook

Playbook

A Step-By-Step Guide To Bring Your Ideas To Life

D. Peterson, Ed.S.

D. Peterson, Ed.S.

Copyright © 2024, D'Undray Peterson

All rights reserved. This book or any portion thereof may not be reproduced or used in any manner whatsoever without the express written permission of the publisher except for the use of brief quotations in a book review or scholarly journal.

ISBN : 9798300008031

Go Get It Publishing, LLC
Tuscaloosa, Alabama

ACKNOWLEDGMENTS

First and foremost, I want to express my deepest gratitude to my family—my amazing wife and our two boys—for their unwavering support and love. Without their encouragement, patience, and understanding, this book would not have been possible. They inspire me every day to keep pushing forward and to dream bigger.

I would also like to extend my heartfelt thanks to the many entrepreneurs I have had the privilege of working with and impacting along the way. Your dedication, passion, and resilience are constant reminders of why I do what I do. This book is as much yours as it is mine, and I am grateful for every lesson and every moment shared with you.

To my mentors, colleagues, and business partners—your guidance and support have played an instrumental role in shaping both my career and this book. Thank you for believing in me and helping me grow along the way.

Lastly, to anyone who has ever taken the leap into entrepreneurship, may this book serve as a source of inspiration, guidance, and empowerment as you build your own path to success.

D. Peterson, Ed.S.

FOREWORD

It is with great pleasure and excitement that I introduce you to "The Idea Execution Playbook," written by D'Undray Peterson. Over the years, I have had the privilege of working with countless entrepreneurs, and I can confidently say that D'Undray stands out as one of the most driven, innovative, and insightful individuals in the field of business development. His journey has been nothing short of inspiring, and this book is the culmination of his wealth of experience, dedication, and relentless pursuit of excellence.

D'Undray is the type of entrepreneur who not only dreams big but also knows how to turn those dreams into tangible results. His expertise spans various industries, and what sets him apart is his deep understanding of the entrepreneurial process—particularly the often-overlooked yet crucial step of execution. Having worked with D'Undray firsthand, I've seen how he approaches business challenges with creativity, resilience, and a clear, methodical approach to turning ideas into reality. His insights have helped countless individuals transform their concepts into thriving businesses, and now, with this book, he's sharing those lessons with you.

While many entrepreneurs focus on ideation, D'Undray has consistently demonstrated a rare talent for executing ideas effectively. He has walked the path from concept to implementation and understands the nuances, the struggles, and the rewards that come with it. This playbook is not just a guide; it's a roadmap shaped by years of trial and error, success and failure, and a deep commitment to seeing others succeed.

If you've ever felt stuck in the gap between having a great idea and bringing it to life, this book is for you. D'Undray's approach is clear, actionable, and rooted in real-world experience. He has distilled his knowledge into a step-by-step framework that will help you navigate the challenges of entrepreneurship and bring your ideas to fruition with confidence.

As you read through these pages, you'll find that his authenticity shines through. He isn't offering a shortcut to success; instead, he provides the tools and mindset necessary to put in the work and execute with precision. His journey and his lessons are a testament to the power of persistence and the incredible possibilities that unfold when you take action.

This playbook is more than just a guide—it's an invitation to unlock your potential, take bold steps, and bring your vision to life. And there's no one better equipped to guide you on this journey than D'Undray Peterson.

So, as you turn the pages and dive into the process of taking your ideas from concept to execution, know that you are in capable hands. D'Undray has walked the path, and now he's here to guide you.

Welcome to "The Idea Execution Playbook." The journey to turning your dreams into reality begins now.

— Mansfield Key III

Growth Development Strategist

D. Peterson, Ed.S.

TABLE OF CONTENTS

PREFACE

Welcome to "The Idea Execution Playbook"! I am thrilled to have you embark on this transformative journey with me. This book is the culmination of my years of experience as an entrepreneur and business consultant, and it is my sincere hope that it will empower and inspire you to bring your ideas to life.

Throughout my career, I have encountered countless individuals who possess immense creativity and passion, yet struggle to navigate the complex path from ideation to execution. I have seen the frustration and disappointment that comes from having brilliant ideas that never reach their full potential. I have witnessed the struggles and setbacks that entrepreneurs face when trying to turn their concepts into successful ventures.

It was from these experiences and interactions that the idea for this book was born. I wanted to create a comprehensive resource that would provide individuals like you with the knowledge, tools, and guidance needed to bridge the gap between idea and implementation. I wanted to demystify the process and equip you with the skills necessary to bring your dreams to fruition.

"The Idea Execution Playbook" is not a magic formula for overnight success. It is a practical roadmap that will require dedication, hard work, and a willingness to learn and adapt. It will challenge you to step out of your comfort zone and confront the obstacles that stand in your way. But I assure you, the rewards that await you on the other side are immeasurable.

Within the pages of this book, you will find a wealth of insights, strategies, and practical advice. I have poured my heart and soul into distilling my experiences, lessons learned, and best practices into a format that is accessible and actionable. Each chapter is designed to provide you with a roadmap to follow and exercises to apply the concepts to your unique situation.

But beyond the practical guidance, I want this book to serve as a source of inspiration. I want you to believe in the power of your ideas and recognize your ability to bring them to life. I want you to embrace the entrepreneurial spirit within you and embark on this journey with confidence and resilience. I want you to know that you are not alone and that others have walked this path before you and are rooting for your success.

Remember, turning an idea into reality is not a solitary endeavor. It requires a community of support, guidance, and collaboration. As you delve into the pages of this book, I encourage you to seek out mentors, connect with fellow entrepreneurs, and engage in conversations that will challenge and enrich your understanding. Together, we can create a network of individuals driven by a shared purpose: to turn ideas into impactful realities.

So, are you ready to transform your ideas into tangible

achievements? Are you ready to take the leap and embark on this thrilling adventure? If so, let us begin. Flip the page, embrace the unknown, and let "The Idea Execution Playbook" be your guide as you embark on this exciting journey of turning your dreams into reality.

INTRODUCTION

Are you tired of having great ideas that never see the light of day? Do you struggle to turn your concepts into successful ventures? If so, this book is for you. "The Idea Execution Playbook" is a step-by-step guide that will help you turn your ideas into reality.

Throughout my journey as an entrepreneur and business consultant, I have encountered countless individuals who possessed incredible ideas but didn't know where to start when it came to bringing those ideas to life. They were filled with passion and creativity, yet lacked the knowledge and direction needed to transform their concepts into tangible achievements.

"The Idea Execution Playbook" was written with these individuals in mind. Whether you're a budding entrepreneur, an aspiring inventor, or a creative professional seeking to turn your dreams into reality, this book is designed to provide you with the guidance and tools necessary to navigate the challenging path from idea to implementation.

In the pages that follow, you will find a comprehensive overview of the entire idea-to-implementation process. From generating innovative ideas to evaluating their potential and transforming them into concrete concepts, to building a minimum viable product, seeking funding, and ultimately launching your product, this book covers it all.

But this book is not just a compilation of theoretical concepts. It is a practical guide that will equip you with the skills and knowledge needed to take action. You will learn techniques for conducting market research and analysis, discovering your target audience, and understanding their needs and desires. You will explore strategies for building a brand and establishing a strong brand identity that resonates with your customers. Additionally, you will gain insights into scaling your business and expanding your reach.

"The Idea Execution Playbook" also addresses the common challenges faced by entrepreneurs and offers valuable advice on problem-solving, decision-making, and overcoming obstacles. It emphasizes the importance of perseverance and resilience in the face of adversity and provides guidance on how to pivot and adapt when necessary. It acknowledges that failure is a natural part of the journey and teaches you how to embrace it as an opportunity for growth and improvement.

Whether you're just starting on your entrepreneurial journey or looking to take your business to the next level, "The Idea Execution Playbook" is your ultimate guide to success. Let this book be your companion as you embark on the exhilarating and challenging path of turning your ideas into reality.

PLAY 1 IDEA GENERATION

Generating new and innovative ideas is a key component of the journey from idea to implementation. Here are some techniques that can be used to spark creativity and generate new ideas:

Brainstorming: This is a group activity where people gather together to come up with as many ideas as possible in a short period of time. Brainstorming can be done individually or in a group and can be a great way to generate a large number of ideas quickly.

Mind Mapping: This technique involves creating a visual representation of your ideas, and connecting related thoughts and concepts. Mind mapping can help to uncover new ideas and make connections between seemingly disparate concepts.

Reverse Engineering: This technique involves taking an existing product or service and coming up with ways to improve it or make it more innovative. This approach can lead to new and unique ideas that solve existing problems in new and creative ways.

Challenge Assumptions: Questioning assumptions and looking for ways to do things differently can lead to new and innovative ideas. This can involve exploring alternative perspectives and pushing the boundaries of what is considered possible.

Take Inspiration from Other Fields: Cross-pollination of ideas from different fields can lead to new and innovative solutions. Looking at how problems are solved in other industries or disciplines can provide fresh perspectives and inspire new ideas.

Keep a Journal: Keeping a journal can be a great way to capture ideas as they come to you. Writing down thoughts, observations, and experiences can provide a source of inspiration and help to trigger new ideas.

Collaboration: Collaborating with others can lead to new and innovative ideas. Working with a team can provide a range of perspectives and help to uncover new ideas that may have been missed working alone.

These are just a few of the many techniques that can be used to generate new and innovative ideas. By using a combination of these techniques and staying open to new experiences and perspectives, individuals can increase their chances of coming up with new and unique ideas.

Now that you've generated your idea, evaluating the potential of an idea is a crucial step on the path to transforming it into a reality. It is during this assessment phase that we determine the viability and feasibility of our concepts, helping us make informed decisions and charting a course toward success. When evaluating the potential of an idea, several factors come into play, each offering valuable insights and considerations. From market demand and competition analysis to assessing resource requirements and scalability, understanding these key elements allows us to determine the likelihood of our idea thriving in the real world. In this section, we will explore some of these critical factors and delve into the thought processes and methodologies necessary to evaluate the potential of your idea effectively. By mastering this skill, you will be equipped with the knowledge and tools needed to make informed decisions that can significantly impact the trajectory of your entrepreneurial journey. Here are some factors to consider when evaluating the potential of an idea:

Market demand: Is there a market for the idea? Can you identify the target audience and determine if there is sufficient demand for the product or service?

Competitor analysis: Who are the competitors in the market and what is their market share? Is the idea differentiated enough to stand out in the market?

Feasibility: Can the idea be realistically implemented given the resources available? Are there any technical or financial barriers to bringing the idea to life?

Scalability: Can the idea be scaled up if successful? Will it have the potential for long-term growth and sustainability?

Alignment with personal and business goals: Does the idea align with your personal and business goals and values? Will pursuing the idea bring you closer to achieving your goals?

Intellectual property: Has the idea been patented or copyrighted by someone else? Do you have the right to use the idea?

Passion and expertise: Are you passionate about the idea and do you have the expertise to bring it to life? Pursuing an idea that you are not passionate about or do not have the necessary skills to implement is likely to lead to burnout and frustration.

Financial viability: Can the idea generate sufficient revenue to cover its costs and provide a return on investment? Can you create a realistic financial model to support the idea?

These are just some of the factors to consider when evaluating the potential of an idea. It is important to be realistic and objective when evaluating an idea and to be willing to abandon an idea if it does not meet your criteria for success. On the other hand, if the idea meets all of your criteria, it may be worth pursuing as it has the potential to bring significant benefits to your life and business.

This step can be summarized with the following acronym:

INSPIRE

Innovation Techniques: Utilize brainstorming, mind mapping, and reverse engineering to ignite creativity.

New Perspectives: Challenge assumptions and draw inspiration from other fields to fuel fresh ideas.

Sharing and Collaboration: Work with others to uncover new angles and unique concepts.

Project Journal: Document ideas regularly to capture inspiration and insights.

Idea Evaluation: Assess market demand, competition, scalability, and feasibility.

Realistic Alignment: Ensure the idea aligns with personal and business goals.

Expertise and Passion: Confirm you have the skills and enthusiasm to bring the idea to life.

Mental Work

As you move through the ideation phase, your mind buzzes with possibilities and potential challenges. Generating new ideas requires a blend of creativity and strategic thinking, pushing you to explore brainstorming techniques like mind mapping and reverse engineering. This mental work is exhilarating yet intense, as you challenge assumptions and experiment with alternative perspectives to ignite fresh concepts. You're caught between excitement and caution, knowing that an innovative idea could make a real-world impact, yet also aware that each idea must withstand rigorous testing and refinement.

When you enter the evaluation phase, your mental focus shifts toward critical analysis. You start by assessing market demand, analyzing competitors, and thinking about scalability—all while considering the feasibility and alignment of the idea with your goals. Your thoughts become more methodical as you examine whether this concept fits with your resources and your business trajectory. You ask yourself whether you have the skills and the passion to see this through and whether the idea has a clear path to success. It's a delicate balance between maintaining the initial excitement and grounding it in market realities and personal objectives.

Finally, as you prepare for implementation, your mental work centers on refining and committing. You focus on financial viability, potential risks, and creating a realistic plan that makes sense both financially and operationally. You consider whether this idea aligns with your personal values and business goals, knowing that only an idea that fits these deeply will sustain you for the long haul. At this stage, you move between enthusiasm and realism, ready to fully commit if the idea passes all tests. This process builds your confidence and transforms your raw concept into a strategic blueprint for action.

PLAY 2 CONCEPT DEVELOPMENT

Turning ideas into concrete concepts is an important step in the process of taking an idea from concept to reality. Here are some steps to help turn an idea into a concrete concept:

Define the problem: Clearly define the problem that the idea is trying to solve. This will help to focus the idea and ensure that it addresses a real need in the market.

Conduct market research: Gather information about the market and potential customers to validate the idea and ensure that there is demand for the solution.

Develop a prototype: Create a working model of the idea to help demonstrate how it works and validate the concept. This can be as simple as a sketch or a more complex model that incorporates key features and functionalities.

Conduct customer validation: Gather feedback from potential customers to validate the concept and refine the idea based on their feedback.

Refine the concept: Based on feedback from market research and customer validation, refine the concept to ensure that it is aligned with market needs and meets customer requirements.

Create a business plan: Develop a comprehensive business plan that outlines the key elements of the concept, including the target market, value proposition, marketing strategy, and financial projections.

Secure funding: Depending on the size and scope of the project, secure the necessary funding to bring the idea to life. This may involve securing investment, securing a loan, or bootstrapping the project using personal funds.

Build and launch: Build the product or service based on the refined concept and launch it in the market. This may involve hiring a team, building partnerships, and establishing a distribution network.

These are just some of the steps involved in turning ideas into concrete concepts. By following a structured approach, you can increase your chances of success and bring your ideas to life in a tangible and impactful way.

One crucial step in this process is defining the vision, mission, and values of your concept. By clearly articulating these foundational elements, you lay the groundwork for a strong and purpose-driven venture. Let's explore the steps and strategies that will help you define and align your vision, mission, and values with your idea, setting the stage for a compelling and impactful implementation.

Vision: The vision is a statement that describes the future state that the concept aims to create. It should be bold, inspiring, and provide a clear picture of what success will look like. A vision statement should be memorable, concise, and convey the purpose of the concept.

Mission: The mission is a statement that describes the purpose of the concept and the role it plays in achieving the vision. The mission should be specific, measurable, and achievable and should provide a clear roadmap for the development and growth of the concept.

Values: The values are the guiding principles that drive the behavior of the concept and its stakeholders. They should be authentic, reflective of the vision and mission, and serve as a touchstone for decision-making.

Having a clear vision, mission, and values helps to focus the concept and ensures that everyone involved is aligned and working towards the same goals. It also provides a framework for making decisions and ensuring that the concept stays true to its purpose and values.

It's important to note that the vision, mission, and values should be reviewed and updated periodically to ensure that they remain relevant and aligned with the changing needs of the market and the concept's stakeholders. This will help to ensure the continued success and growth of the concept.

This step can be summarized with the following acronyms:

I - Identify the Problem: Define the problem your idea addresses to focus on solving a real need.

D - Do Market Research: Understand the market and validate demand through research and customer insights.

E - Envision a Prototype: Develop a model to showcase how your idea works and test the concept.

A - Align with Customer Feedback: Use customer validation to refine and ensure market alignment.

V - Vision Statement: Articulate a bold, clear vision that captures the concept's purpose and future impact.

I - Integrate the Mission: Define the purpose and roadmap that guides the concept toward the vision.

S - Set Core Values: Establish guiding principles that drive decision-making and behavior.

I - Implement the Business Plan: Outline key elements, target market, value proposition, and financial projections.

O - Obtain Funding: Secure necessary funding or resources to bring the concept to life.

N - **Navigate the Launch**: Build, launch, and establish partnerships to introduce the concept to the market.

Mental Work

When you begin the journey of turning an idea into a concrete concept, your mind often feels like a wellspring of possibilities, buzzing with both excitement and uncertainty. Defining the problem is your anchor; it's where you mentally connect with the specific challenge you're trying to solve. At this stage, you're narrowing your focus, envisioning how your idea meets a real need, and ensuring it has substance. Your mental energy shifts toward validating the market and understanding customer needs, as you immerse yourself in research and insights that will help ground your idea in reality.

As you develop a prototype, your mind shifts from abstract to tangible. You're envisioning the concept's structure, seeing how it could work, and considering how to create a working model. There's a mix of creative freedom and practical restraint here, as you want the prototype to be both inspiring and viable. Gathering customer feedback becomes essential, and your mind stays open to refining the idea based on their experiences. This process can be challenging, as you balance your original vision with feedback that might push you to adapt in ways you hadn't anticipated. But every suggestion or observation from a potential customer feeds your insight, and you see your concept becoming more aligned with what people genuinely need and want.

With a refined concept in hand, you're mentally ready to focus on formalizing the vision, mission, and values. This is where you create a framework for your concept that others can rally around. Your mind is now in alignment mode, thinking about long-term strategy, business planning, and securing the resources necessary to launch. This mental work demands clarity and commitment as you develop a business plan, secure funding, and prepare for launch. It's a blend of focused energy and flexible strategy as you make sure every aspect, from vision to values, connects cohesively with your goal. By the time you're ready to launch, your mind is equipped with a structured blueprint, confident and ready to turn your concept into reality.

PLAY 3 MARKET RESEARCH

Understanding your target audience is crucial to the success of any concept. It allows you to tailor your product or service to meet the specific needs and wants of your customers, and to effectively market and sell your concept to them. Here are the steps to understand your target audience:

Define your target audience: Start by defining the specific group of people who are most likely to be interested in your product or service. Consider factors such as age, income, location, education, and interests when defining your target audience.

Conduct market research: Gather data on your target audience by conducting market research. This can include surveys, focus groups, and online research. This will give you a deeper understanding of your target audience, including their needs, wants, and behaviors.

Create buyer personas: Use the information gathered from market research to create buyer personas. A buyer persona is a fictional representation of your ideal customer and should include information on demographics, motivations, and pain points.

Analyze competitors: Analyze your competitors to understand how they are serving your target audience and what their strengths and weaknesses are. This information can help you to differentiate your product or service and to identify growth opportunities.

Monitor customer feedback: Continuously gather feedback from your target audience to ensure that your product or service is meeting their needs and to identify areas for improvement. This can include customer surveys, reviews, and social media feedback.

By understanding your target audience, you can develop a product or service that is tailored to their needs and wants and create a marketing and sales strategy that is effective in reaching and selling to them. This will increase the chances of success and ensure that your concept is well-received by the market. Conducting market research and analysis is an important step in taking an idea from concept to reality. It helps to validate the idea, understand the target market, and determine the potential for success. Here are the steps to conduct market research and analysis:

Define the research objective: Start by defining the objective of the research. This will guide the research process and help to ensure that the information gathered is relevant and useful.

Identify data sources: Determine the best sources of data to gather information on the market, the target audience, and the competition. This can include primary research (such as surveys and focus groups) and secondary research (such as industry reports and online research).

Gather data: Collect data using the sources identified in step 2. Ensure that the data is reliable and relevant to the research objective.

Analyze the data: Once the data has been gathered, analyze it to identify patterns, trends, and insights. This can include statistical analysis, trend analysis, and segmentation analysis.

Test the concept: Use the information gathered from the market research to validate the concept and to identify any potential challenges. This can include conducting small-scale tests or pilot projects to see how the concept performs in the real world.

Market research and analysis is an iterative process and should be conducted regularly to ensure that the information gathered is up-to-date and relevant. By conducting market research and analysis, individuals and businesses can gain a deeper understanding of the market and the target audience, and make informed decisions about the development and growth of the concept.

Evaluating the competition and market demand is an important step in taking an idea from concept to reality. It helps to identify opportunities and threats in the market and to determine the potential for success. Here are the steps to evaluate the competition and market demand:

Identify the competition: Determine who the competitors are in the market and what they offer. This can include direct competitors (who offer similar products or services) and indirect competitors (who offer alternative solutions to the same problem).

Assess market demand: Assess the demand for the product or service in the market. This can include conducting market research to gather information on the target audience and their needs and wants.

Identify market trends: Identify trends in the market that may impact the demand for the product or service. This can include demographic changes, technological advancements, and shifts in consumer behavior.

Determine market size: Determine the size of the market and the growth potential. This will help to determine the potential for success and the resources required to enter and compete in the market.

By evaluating the competition and market demand, individuals and businesses can gain a deeper understanding of the market and the potential for success. This information can be used to make informed decisions about the development and growth of the concept and to identify opportunities for differentiation and competitive advantage.

This step can be summarized with the following acronym:

AIM TEST stands for:

Audience Definition: Identify and define your target group.

Insight Gathering: Conduct market research to understand their needs.

Market Analysis: Examine competitors and identify gaps.

Target Persona Creation: Build buyer personas based on gathered insights.

Evaluate Market Demand: Assess the market size and growth potential.

Study Competitor Landscape: Analyze competition strengths and weaknesses.

Test and Monitor: Continuously test the concept, gather feedback, and improve.

Mental Work

In market research, your mind focuses on understanding people—who they are, what they need, and how they interact with the world around them. The first step, defining your target audience, requires you to imagine the lives of potential customers: their age, location, interests, and daily challenges. You're building a mental profile of the people most likely to connect with your product or service. As you conduct market research, gathering data through surveys, focus groups, or online research, your mind shifts from imagining to observing. The feedback you collect informs and sharpens your understanding, allowing you to see patterns and trends emerge within your target audience.

Creating buyer personas deepens this mental work. You're now stepping into the shoes of your ideal customers, envisioning their motivations, needs, and frustrations. This exercise allows you to empathize with your audience, making their journey personal as you think about how your concept can offer them solutions. Analyzing competitors also plays a key role in refining your approach, giving you insights into how others are reaching similar customers and what you can do differently to stand out. It's a strategic comparison that allows you to identify strengths to build on and gaps to fill.

Throughout this process, your mind is agile, adapting based on customer feedback, which you gather continuously. Whether it's surveys, reviews, or social media interactions, every piece of feedback shapes and refines your concept to better meet market demands. By continuously testing and monitoring, you're both validating your concept and staying in tune with shifts in customer expectations and behaviors. This mental engagement ensures that your concept doesn't just meet initial goals but evolves with the audience's changing needs and preferences.

Market research is an ongoing commitment to understanding and adapting. As you gather insights, analyze competitors, and test your concept, your mind remains in a feedback loop, dedicated to learning and refining to increase your chances of success. This iterative process—Define, Research, Analyze, and Refine— transforms your concept from an abstract idea into a well-aligned offering ready for real-world impact.

PLAY 4 SERVICE/PRODUCT DEVELOPMENT

Bringing an idea for a new service or concept to life often begins by creating and testing a prototype. This process allows you to see how your service might work in the real world, gather feedback, and make improvements before a full-scale launch.

Steps to Bring Your Service to Life:

Outline Your Service Concept: Start by defining the basics of your service. Who will it serve, and what problem does it solve? Describe what the service should accomplish and what aspects you want to test, like customer experience, ease of use, or any potential challenges.

Map Out the Experience: Create a rough plan of how your service will work. This could include sketching out the process on paper or using simple tools to visualize the customer journey. Imagine each step your customer will take, from their first interaction with the service to the end result.

Create a Test Version (Prototype): Develop a basic version of your service that allows you to test it on a small scale. For a service, this might involve setting up a pilot run with a few select participants. The goal is to keep things simple, focusing on the core aspects rather than making everything perfect.

Gather Feedback from Users: Run the service prototype with real users and ask for their honest feedback. This could be in the form of casual conversations, surveys, or even one-on-one interviews. Observing people as they go through the process can reveal what's working well and what's confusing or frustrating.

Review and Adjust: Take note of any common issues or useful suggestions from your feedback. Maybe users found certain steps too complicated, or perhaps they offered ideas on additional features. Prioritize these improvements based on their impact on the overall experience.

Refine and Retest: Make adjustments to your service based on the feedback and try it again. Each test run allows you to improve the service until it's smooth and effective. This step-by-step refinement process makes sure that by the time you launch, your service feels polished and ready.

Launch Your Service: Once you're confident in your service, you're ready to introduce it to a wider audience. Start with a soft launch to gradually grow awareness, and continue to engage with users to keep improving.

The process doesn't end with the launch. Continue gathering feedback from customers, make updates, and keep refining your service. This approach not only helps ensure your service meets people's needs but also lets you adapt as those needs evolve.

With each round of testing and feedback, you bring your idea closer to its full potential, making it a service that truly resonates with your audience.

This step can be summarized with the following acronym:

P.R.O.T.O.T.Y.P.E.

Plan Your Concept: Define the service, its purpose, and its audience.

Rough Outline: Map out the customer experience from start to finish.

Organize Prototype: Build a simple, testable version of the service.

Test with Users: Gather honest feedback from real users.

Observe & Adjust: Note common issues and refine the service.

Tune & Retest: Make changes based on feedback and try again.

Yield Results: Move toward a polished version of the service.

Prepare to Launch: Roll out your service with a soft launch.

Evolve Continuously: Keep gathering feedback and improving.

This **P.R.O.T.O.T.Y.P.E.** method ensures a structured path from idea to impactful, customer-focused service.

Mental Work

Developing a new service or product begins with clarifying your idea and imagining how it will come to life in the real world. The first step, outlining your service concept, challenges your mind to think about the problem you're solving, who you're solving it for, and how your solution will make a difference. You must envision the service's goals, how it will function, and what customer experiences are most important to test. Here, your mind is preparing for an iterative process of refining and improving based on real-world feedback.

Mapping out the experience requires you to visualize the customer's journey from start to finish. This mental exercise brings clarity to your service design as you plan out each step of the process. It requires you to think about the user's emotional journey—what they'll feel at each stage—and how you can make each interaction as smooth and impactful as possible. Creating a rough outline, even if just sketched out on paper, helps you focus on the big picture, allowing you to mentally see how different components of the service fit together.

When you create your prototype, your mental work shifts to problem-solving. This is where you simplify the service into its core elements, making it manageable and testable. Here, your mind is focused on how to execute a small-scale version of your idea, recognizing that it doesn't need to be perfect—just functional enough to learn from real users. As you run your test, your mental approach should be observant, paying attention to what users experience, what they struggle with, and how they react.

Gathering feedback requires active listening and empathy. Your mind will be tuned to understand both the spoken and unspoken responses of your users—what they like, what they find confusing, and what they suggest to improve the experience. This feedback process is crucial, as it offers insight into the gaps between your vision and the reality of customer needs. It's a time for reflection and adjustment, where your mind is processing critical data that will refine your service.

Reviewing and adjusting the service based on feedback involves analytical thinking. You'll mentally sift through the issues and prioritize solutions that have the greatest impact on the user experience. It's about understanding where the most significant improvements can be made and which changes will make the service flow better. The refinement process may take several iterations, each time requiring you to synthesize feedback and fine-tune your service to make it seamless.

As you approach the final stages, the mental work moves toward the preparation of a polished, ready-to-launch service. You'll mentally anticipate how your audience will react and be prepared to monitor their feedback even after the launch. Even after going live, your work isn't done; your mind will continue to focus on listening to customers, evaluating their feedback, and adapting as needed. This ongoing mental engagement ensures that your service grows and evolves in response to the ever-changing needs of your audience.

Using the P.R.O.T.O.T.Y.P.E. method keeps your mind structured and focused on the goal of delivering a service that is constantly evolving based on user feedback. From planning and testing to refinement and continuous improvement, this process helps you stay agile, informed, and ready to deliver a service that resonates deeply with your audience.

PLAY 5 HOME-BASED CEO: 50 LOW-COST BUSINESS IDEAS TO GET YOU STARTED

Now that we've gone through the process of taking your ideas from concept to execution, it's time to shift gears and put those principles into action. For those who may need a little extra inspiration or a proven path to follow, here are some business ideas that require minimal upfront investment and can be operated from the comfort of your own home. While there are countless opportunities to explore, we'll focus on 50 great options, with a special emphasis on financial services and life insurance—industries that I am personally passionate about and actively involved in. It is also the 2nd most profitable industry in the US as of the writing of this book. Let's dive into these opportunities that can help you take the next step toward becoming a successful Home-Based CEO.

1. Life Insurance Brokerage

Investment Needed: Low to Moderate (Licensing) Build a life insurance brokerage firm where you work with multiple insurance carriers to offer a wide range of products. You can work from home, but it requires a strong understanding of the market and products.

2. Financial Planner

Investment Needed: Low to Moderate (Certifications) Help clients with financial planning, retirement strategies, and investment management. With minimal upfront costs, you can start a financial planning service that operates virtually, helping clients achieve financial goals.

3. Credit Repair Consultant

Investment Needed: Low (Certification) Assist individuals with improving their credit scores by disputing errors, providing education on financial literacy, and helping them manage their debt. Credit repair businesses are always in demand.

4. Tax Preparation

Investment Needed: Low (Software and Training) Offer tax preparation services to individuals and small businesses. You can provide these services remotely or locally, using tax software and staying current with IRS regulations.

5. Mortgage Broker

Investment Needed: Moderate (Licensing) Become a licensed mortgage broker and help people find the best mortgage rates and loan programs. Many brokers work from home, utilizing online platforms to connect with clients.

6. Business Consultant

Investment Needed: Low (Experience/Expertise) Offer your expertise to other businesses by providing strategic advice, growth solutions, and operational improvements. This can be done remotely through calls or video conferencing.

7. Virtual Assistant

Investment Needed: Low (No formal training required) Provide administrative support services such as email management, scheduling, data entry, and social media management to busy professionals. This is a scalable home business with minimal costs.

8. Affiliate Marketer

Investment Needed: Low (Website, Marketing) Promote products or services online and earn commissions on sales made through your affiliate links. The financial and health-related products niche can be particularly profitable.

9. Online Course Creator

Investment Needed: Low to Moderate (Course Creation Tools) Create and sell online courses that teach others about personal finance, insurance, investing, or even life skills. Platforms like Teachable or Udemy make it easy to launch your course.

10. Bookkeeping

Investment Needed: Low (Accounting Software) Offer bookkeeping services to small businesses, helping them maintain accurate financial records. With the rise of cloud-based accounting software, this is an easy business to run remotely.

11. Social Media Manager

Investment Needed: Low (Computer and Tools) Help businesses build their online presence by managing their social media accounts. Many small businesses and entrepreneurs need this service, which can easily be done from home.

12. Content Writer

Investment Needed: Low (Computer and Internet Access) If you have a knack for writing, start offering content writing services. You can write blogs, articles, newsletters, and more for businesses in the financial sector or other industries.

13. Event Planner

Investment Needed: Low to Moderate (Marketing and Software) If you're organized and detail-oriented, start a home-based event planning business. Specializing in virtual events or small-scale gatherings is an excellent niche to tap into.

14. Online Retailer (E-commerce)

Investment Needed: Moderate (Inventory, Website) Start an e-commerce business selling products online through platforms like Etsy, eBay, or Shopify. You can focus on niche markets like financial education tools or insurance-related products.

15. Resume Writer

Investment Needed: Low (Marketing) Offer resume writing services to individuals looking to enhance their resumes or LinkedIn profiles. This is a business that can be done entirely from home with minimal investment.

16. Life Coach

Investment Needed: Low to Moderate (Certification) Become a certified life coach and offer coaching services on financial planning, career development, or personal growth. Life coaching can be done virtually, allowing you to reach clients globally.

17. Health Insurance Consultant

Investment Needed: Low (Licensing and Training) Specialize in helping clients navigate the complexities of health insurance plans. As a home-based business, you can consult with clients via phone or video calls.

18. Dropshipping

Investment Needed: Low (Website and Marketing) With dropshipping, you don't need to hold any inventory. You simply act as a middleman between suppliers and customers. Focus on products like financial tools, planners, or educational resources.

19. Online Marketing Consultant

Investment Needed: Low (Experience) Help small businesses and entrepreneurs improve their online marketing efforts. This could include SEO, paid ads, social media strategies, or content marketing.

20. Pet Sitting or Dog Walking

Investment Needed: Low (Liability Insurance) Start a pet-sitting or dog-walking business where you can care for pets while their owners are away. This is a simple, home-based service that's always in demand.

21. Real Estate Investment

Investment Needed: Moderate (Capital) Get into real estate by investing in rental properties or flipping houses. This can be done part-time while working from home, especially if you hire a property manager.

22. Online Marketing Affiliate (Insurance)

Investment Needed: Low (Website, Marketing) Become an affiliate marketer for life insurance products. Promote insurance policies through your blog, social media, or ads, earning commissions for each lead or sale.

23. Home Staging

Investment Needed: Low to Moderate (Supplies and Marketing) Help homeowners and realtors stage homes for sale. You can operate this business from home, offering design consultations and working with sellers.

24. Debt Collection Agency

Investment Needed: Low to Moderate (Licensing) Start a debt collection service from home, helping businesses recover owed funds. While you'll need to be familiar with regulations, it's a profitable and low-cost business to begin.

25. Translation Services

Investment Needed: Low (No Formal Tools Needed) If you're bilingual, offer translation services for documents, websites, or conversations. This is a service that businesses, especially in global finance and insurance, frequently need.

26. Tax Consultant for Small Businesses

Investment Needed: Low (Tax Software) Specialize in tax consulting for small businesses. Offering advice on deductions, tax filings, and tax strategy can be done remotely and with little investment.

27. Stock Market Educator

Investment Needed: Low (Website, Course Platform) Create educational materials or teach online courses about the stock market, investing, and wealth-building strategies.

28. Freelance Designer (Web, Graphic, or Logo)

Investment Needed: Low (Design Software) If you're creative, start a freelance design business creating websites, logos, or marketing materials for clients in various industries, including financial services.

29. Financial Blogger

Investment Needed: Low (Website, Hosting) Create a blog focusing on personal finance, life insurance, or financial literacy. Monetize it through affiliate marketing, sponsored posts, or selling your products.

30. Notary Public

Investment Needed: Low (Certification) Become a certified notary public and offer mobile notary services. This is an essential service that can be done from home, making it an easy business to start.

31. Professional Organizer

Investment Needed: Low (Marketing) Offer home organization services for clients looking to declutter their homes or offices. You can offer virtual consultations or in-person services.

32. Freelance Virtual Bookkeeper

Investment Needed: Low (Accounting Software) If you have bookkeeping skills, offer virtual bookkeeping services to small businesses. You can work from home and set your schedule.

33. Online Fitness Coach

Investment Needed: Low (Certification and Marketing) Offer virtual fitness coaching and nutrition plans. With more people working from home, virtual personal training is in high demand.

34. Insurance Sales Representative

Investment Needed: Low to Moderate (Licensing) Sell a variety of insurance policies, from auto and home to health and life. With a relatively low startup cost, you can begin as an independent agent.

35. Wedding Planner

Investment Needed: Low (Marketing and Networking) Specialize in wedding planning from home, offering virtual consultations and vendor coordination.

36. Mobile Car Wash and Detailing

Investment Needed: Low (Supplies and Marketing) Start a mobile car wash and detailing service, where you clean vehicles at your client's location.

37. Video Production Services

Investment Needed: Moderate (Camera Equipment) Start a video production service for online businesses, offering everything from promotional videos to educational content.

38. Resume Coach

Investment Needed: Low (Website and Marketing) Help job seekers improve their resumes and prepare for interviews. You can offer one-on-one sessions via video call.

39. Influencer Marketing Consultant

Investment Needed: Low (Experience and Social Media Tools) If you're experienced in social media marketing, work as a consultant to help brands connect with influencers in the financial or insurance sectors.

40. Online Travel Agent

Investment Needed: Low (Training and Certification) Become a travel agent specializing in booking vacations, flights, and accommodations. You can cater to clients looking for affordable, stress-free travel planning.

41. Pet Products E-commerce Store

Investment Needed: Low (Inventory, Website) Create an online store selling pet-related products like grooming supplies, toys, and accessories.

42. DIY Craft Seller

Investment Needed: Low (Materials) Start a craft-based business selling handmade products like jewelry, home decor, or apparel on platforms like Etsy.

43. Personal Shopper

Investment Needed: Low (Marketing) Offer personal shopping services, from groceries to clothing. This is a growing trend, especially for time-starved individuals.

44. Mobile App Developer

Investment Needed: Moderate (Development Tools) Develop mobile apps, focusing on areas like financial management or health. You can start small with simple apps and expand.

45. Custom Furniture Maker

Investment Needed: Moderate (Tools and Materials) Start a business creating custom furniture. Focus on small items that don't require a huge workshop, or sell online for local delivery.

46. Subscription Box Service

Investment Needed: Low to Moderate (Products and Packaging) Start a subscription box service focused on a niche like health, beauty, or finance. You can curate monthly themed products delivered to subscribers.

47. Voiceover Artist

Investment Needed: Low (Recording Equipment) Use your voice for voiceover work in commercials, animations, or instructional videos. This is a great business you can run from home.

48. Mobile App Developer for Financial Tools

Investment Needed: Moderate (Development) If you have programming skills, develop financial tools such as budget trackers or expense management apps.

49. Debt Counselor

Investment Needed: Low (Training) Offer financial advice on reducing debt, negotiating settlements, and managing personal finances. You can work with clients remotely to help them regain financial stability.

49. Debt Counselor

Investment Needed: Low (Training) Offer financial advice on reducing debt, negotiating settlements, and managing personal finances. You can work with clients remotely to help them regain financial stability.

50. Financial Blogger/Influencer

Investment Needed: Low (Website and Content Creation Tools) If you have a passion for personal finance, life insurance, or wealth-building strategies, start a financial blog or become an influencer on platforms like Instagram or YouTube. Share tips, advice, and experiences with your audience, and monetize through affiliate marketing, sponsored content, or offering your products, such as e-books or courses. This is a great way to leverage your expertise and create a passive income stream while working from home.

ABOUT THE AUTHOR

D'Undray Peterson is a seasoned entrepreneur and business leader with over 25 years of experience in launching, managing, and growing successful ventures. Known for his innovative mindset and relentless drive, D'Undray has built a strong reputation in the world of entrepreneurship as a forward-thinking leader who is unafraid to challenge norms and inspire others to do the same.

Beyond his own business endeavors, D'Undray is a sought-after speaker and thought leader, frequently presenting at conferences, workshops, and events across the country. His talks are known for their actionable insights and motivational approach, leaving audiences equipped and inspired.

In *The Idea Execution Playbook*, D'Undray brings together years of experience and expertise to guide aspiring and established entrepreneurs alike. This book is packed with practical strategies, real-life examples, and inspiring stories designed to help readers bridge the gap between idea and execution. Whether you're looking to start your own business or elevate an existing one, this playbook offers essential advice for every stage of the journey.

For more resources, insights, and to stay connected, visit dtpeterson.com.

D. Peterson, Ed.S.

Made in the USA
Columbia, SC
27 November 2024

47331220R00033